Blank Sheet Music For Piano

: Staff Paper Musicians Notebook

12 stave 104Pages / 8x10inch

(Composition Books - Music Manuscript Paper)

Ella Ruby

Published by PUBLISHING COMPANY in 2016

First edition: First printing

Illustrations and design © 2016 T.Michelle

Author Contact

https://www.facebook.com/groups/1523056898003358/

ISBN-13: 978-1541388819

ISBN-10: 154138881X

Thank you

Hope you've enjoyed your reading experience.

We here at T.Michelle will always strive to deliver to you the highest quality guides.

So I'd like to thank you for supporting us and reading until the very end.

Before you go, would you mind leaving us a review on Amazon?

It will mean a lot to us and support us creating high quality guides for you in the future.

Thanks once again and here's where you can leave a review.

Get Free Ebook Coloring Page below

https://www.facebook.com/groups/1523056898003358/

Warmly yours,

T.Michelle's Team